Dr. S♥nya Says
L♥ve Yourself First Everyday

30 Days of Instant Inspiration

...and other thoughts

DR. SONYA L. FORD

Copyright © 2012 Dr. Sonya L. Ford

All rights reserved.

ISBN-13: 978-1475154399
ISBN-10: 1475154399

DEDICATION

This book is dedicated to all who believed in me
and encouraged me to live my life to the fullest
in spite of the obstacles along my path.
Thank you for inspiring me.

INTRODUCTION

Life brings you curve balls everyday. Whether it's the challenges of being a parent, communicating with family and friends, or having a healthy and loving relationship with your significant other, we all need a little L.Y.F.E. support. This book will help you make it through the challenges.

This book will inspire you to
Love Yourself First Everyday!

It's not being selfish.
It's self-preservation.

ACKNOWLEDGMENTS

Sincerest thanks to my **family** and **friends** for always being there. A special thanks to my "**other mothers** and **fathers**" for teaching me patience and showing me the light at the end of the long, dark tunnel. To my **sister-friends** – words cannot express my l♥ve for each of you – you know who you are!!! Dr. **Flip** and Ren**Nash** – YOU ROCK! To the Ladies of Delta Sigma Theta Sorority, Inc. – thank you for inspiring me. To the Fabulous **Fords** (*Mommy and Family in Winchester, Florida, Texas, & beyond*) – you are just that ...*FABULOUS*!

To my **children** – Stanford & Sydnae –
A mother's l♥ve is *everlasting...**know** & **believe*** that!
I l♥ve you to infinity and beyond, beyond

TABLE OF CONTENTS

Day 1   Confronting Bad People

Day 2   Controlling Your Attitude

Day 3   Self-Love

Day 4   Forgiveness

Day 5   Depression

Day 6   Conquering

Day 7   Emotional Rollercoaster

Day 8   Finding Joy

Day 9   Capturing Your Power

Day 10 Fulfilling Your Purpose

Day 11 Motivate Yourself

Day 12 Love Evaluation

Day 13 Quiet Time

Day 14 Release

Day 15 The Power of Words

Day 16	Pulling Weeds
Day 17	Understanding Your Circle
Day 18	Karma
Day 19	Reinvent Yourself
Day 20	Pity Party
Day 21	Doors
Day 22	Taking Me Time
Day 23	Your Today
Day 24	Choices
Day 25	Emotional Bankruptcy
Day 26	Transition
Day 27	The Power of Saying NO
Day 28	Battered but not Broken
Day 29	Un-Friending
Day 30	Stronger

Other Thoughts

DAY 1

Confronting Bad People

Stand up and confront the negative people in your life...

Stop letting others take your kindness for a weakness.

It's okay to be a giver but it's not okay to allow others to use you. You must confront the takers...don't allow them to walk all over you. Stand up...have a backbone...it's not about being mean...it's about respect...command it...demand it.

There are people in this world who simply use others... you've met them...interacted with them...been used by them...but today say "no more" and do not allow the takers to continue taking from you.

Know your limits and know when enough is enough.

DAY 2

Controlling Your Attitude

Often times our attitudes prevent us from that next great thing…whether it be a promotion, a relationship, or an extra discount. Learning to control your attitude is an important attribute. You must always remember that you can't control what others say or do – you can only control how you react to others.

Don't give others power by losing your temper and "going there." Stay in control…let your calmness prevail…you control your attitude…and when you feel a little froggy …don't jump…your calm attitude will wield more power than you could ever believe.

DAY 3

Self-Love

Can you truly love yourself?

Do we always need the approval of others to make ourselves feel better?

Take a long look in the mirror.

What do you see?

Do you feel love for the image looking back at you?

When we learn self-love, the approval of others becomes secondary. Tell yourself – *I love you just the way you are*!

Love your thick thighs, full lips, and sensuous hips. Know you are smart and capable of great things. Only then will the chains of approval from others fall from your wrists. Only then will you be able to feel confident about your daily choices and life decisions.

Love your inner self and your outer self.

DAY 4

Forgiveness

I once read "forgiving someone does not make them right, it sets you free."

Harboring anger toward someone steals the joy from your heart.

Anger can grow so large it overtakes your entire being! You being angry does not affect the person you are angry with. It only keeps you in a constant negative frame of mind and prevents you from seeing the goodness and joy that surrounds you.

Begin to release your anger…you will feel the cloud of hatred lift from your soul. This will allow peace and love to overtake you. You will never forget the hurt that was done to you…but forgiveness will set you free.

Forgive and don't look back…release the bonds of anger …only then will you be free of the hurt.

DAY 5

Depression

People often say to me – "you look so happy…you always have a smile on your face…" – yet they don't see through the mask.

It's important to know that we all have a mask that we wear for others.

We wear the mask to hide the hurt. The things from childhood and adulthood that have caused so much pain …we mask the hurt feelings with a smile or by saying "I'm okay!" Yet the hurt is so deep that in quiet moments, depression slips in.

You cannot change the past…you can't smother the pain and disappointment…but you *can* learn to be victorious over the hurt that hides deep inside. Stop blaming the past and take responsibility for your future happiness.

You must choose to be happy. You must know you are not a victim of the past…you are victorious over the past and can stand now and tell your story of triumph.

DAY 6

Conquering

Domestic Violence is real…

People often associate Domestic Violence with physical abuse; yet the abuse can also be psychological, emotional, sexual, or financial. These abusive tactics are an attempt to wield power in a relationship…often times making excuses for the batterers…saying "it only happened once," "he/she didn't mean it," or "it was an accident."

These excuses are made because of hurt, humiliation, or self-blame. The sad truth is, if it happens once, it will probably happen again.

It's time to erase the victimization tape in your head and begin to claim that you are a conqueror. You must stand up and render the batterers powerless. It may mean starting over…with nothing but the clothes on your back…but it's a fresh start…a powerful statement to proclaim - NO MORE!

STAND UP for yourself. It's time to stop being a victim and become a conqueror.

DAY 7

Emotional Rollercoaster

Loving someone can be exactly like a rollercoaster ride.

Your heart will beat with anticipation for the highs and then sink deep in despair during the lows. There will always be ups and downs. No relationship is perfect.

The important piece is to have more ups then downs. Make a list and evaluate your relationship. See if the happy moments outnumber the sad moments.

You always have a choice. You don't have to settle. You must choose to be emotionally, physically, and mentally healthy.

Don't ignore the red flags because you are afraid of being alone. Take control of you. Choose to be happy. Take a good, hard look at your emotional rollercoaster.

Only you can decide to stay on the ride or get off.

DAY 8

Finding Joy

We all have the ability to experience great JOY in our lives. Yet, we often allow others to steal our JOY and then suffer in silence.

Suffer no more…think of JOY as never ending. The good news is…no matter how many times someone tries to steal your JOY; you have so much more JOY inside of you.

No one can really take your JOY from you unless you allow it. There will be moments where you think there is more rain than sunshine…but after the rain, the sunshine arrives along with a rainbow of JOY.

Know that your JOY is abundant…it may diminish temporarily but it is always there waiting to brighten your day.

Seek JOY and embrace it.

DAY 9

Capturing Your Power

It is difficult to hear *"accept the things you cannot change"* and *"let go and let God"* when you are in the midst of a painful situation.

Oftentimes you cannot see the power and promise you have because of the immediate pain you feel.

Finding strength during challenging times can be difficult. Think of what is on the other side of the pain.

How many times have you come through situations and then looked back and were amazed how you conquered the pain? Each painful situation is yet another reminder of your strength.

You have the power to overcome any unpleasant situation.

Know you have the strength to turn your pain into power.

DAY 10

Fulfilling Your Purpose

We all have a predetermined destiny or purpose. Yet, the daily choices we make either deter our purpose or fulfill our purpose.

It is your choice to let life's circumstances defeat you or to stand up and fight.

You always have a choice. Along the way you will have speed bumps and roadblocks. Yet, you can choose to stay stuck or choose to find a way around your obstacles.

Fulfilling your purpose is a choice.

CHOOSE wisely!

DAY 11

Motivate Yourself

No… Can't… Don't… Won't…

In trying times, negativity can undermine your hopes and dreams.

Only YOU can change the negative energy into positive energy.

Tell yourself - YES…I CAN…I DO…I WILL!

When the entire world seems to be holding you back, dig deep into your soul and be your own cheerleader.

Know you are special!

Know you are loved!

Know you can and you will!

Motivate yourself!

DAY 12

Love Evaluation

When love takes control, you only see the good in your significant other.

Love can be euphoric. Yet, when the rose-colored glasses are taken off, the euphoria is often replaced with a reality check.

This is the time to evaluate your senses, which are often numbed by love. Begin to see the red flags that were so often ignored.

This love-evaluation can go either way. Weigh the pros and cons of the relationship. If your love-evaluation leaves you feeling unsettled, then "I think you better let it go."

Although it may be another "Love T.K.O.," the love-bell will sound again.

You will know when the time is right to get in the love-ring again.

DAY 13

Quiet Time

Whether it's the traffic, the TV, ring tones, music, children, or people; noise is all around us.

In this very busy world, it is important to find a little quiet time.

Time to listen to your thoughts. Time to seek your higher power. Time to relax.

Time for YOU!

Slow down and find a few minutes of silence. It will be refreshing.

You will feel rejuvenated.

Let the peace from within overtake your mind, body, and soul.

DAY 14

Release

Love cannot be one-sided.

When you have given your all and you have nothing left to give, just take a deep breath and then release it.

As you release the air, release the need to hold on tight to what once was there.

Take in another deep breath and breathe in a desire to begin anew.

Release all negative thoughts and hopes for what cannot be and begin to feel the love you have for yourself.

One day love will bloom anew.

Take one last peek at what once was and let it go forever.

DAY 15

The Power of Words

Words have the power to hurt or heal.

As we speak each day, we bring life to the words we use.

These words can invoke so many emotions. A simple word or phrase can have multiple meanings to the recipient.

It is important to think about our intent behind the words we use. Once a word is released from our lips, we cannot retrieve it.

Words are like pebbles thrown in a pond, the reverberation continues long after the pebble has been thrown.

We must choose our words carefully in our daily conversations; knowing when to be direct and when to be diplomatic.

We must monitor our tongues and remember how much power our words really have.

DAY 16

Pulling Weeds

When life seems to have you down, it is often easier to hibernate and pretend the pain within does not exist.

The problems rooted deeply within can be like weeds overwhelming your beautiful garden.

It is often difficult to tackle the weeds all at once. Start small. Tackle one problem at a time. The problems didn't appear all at once and will not disappear all at once.

Like the beautiful garden overrun by weeds, the beauty is still there, you just have to dig deep to see it.

Your joy is still there despite the problems of life. You just have to dig deep past the pain to access it.

The joy is much more powerful than the pain of hurt and disappointment.

Start each day uprooting one problem (weed) in your life and see the joy (beauty) within.

DAY 17

Understanding Your Circle

Who is in your circle?

Our relationships are made of inner and outer circles.

We choose who we allow to be in our innermost circle and who must remain on the fringe.

It is important to constantly reevaluate the relationship of those in our circles. Some are seemingly irreplaceable; yet, others make us question our bond.

We cannot be afraid to erase relationships that cause us pain or add relationships that bring us joy.

Frequently re-evaluate who is in your circle.

DAY 18

Karma

What goes around…comes around…

It is often difficult to refrain from retaliating when you've been wronged. The urge for revenge is often very strong.

Harboring negative feelings toward someone will not lead to peace within your soul. It will only cause more angst.

The best way to protect your heart when you've been wronged is to not let the hurt overtake you. Think of it as a life lesson never to be learned again.

Be above the fray and live your life to the fullest. Your success and happiness is revenge enough for those who wished you ill-will.

The good news is people can be mean-spirited for only so long before the negative energy comes back on them.

Therefore, continue to be the best person you can be and all the good in you will be rewarded.

Harboring ill-will can only bring ill-will. KARMA is very powerful.

DAY 19

Reinvent Yourself

Today is the day to make a fresh start.

On occasion you may want to throw in the towel and give up. Yet, it is at these troubled moments when you have the opportunity to begin anew.

Reevaluate all that appears to be going wrong in your life. Make a list and then begin to tackle each issue one at a time. Take those gentle baby steps and begin to reinvent yourself. You will find the list to be less overwhelming when you look at the issues individually.

Starting small will give you mini-victories and the courage to tackle the bigger issues you may face. The list will begin to dwindle and your self-confidence will begin to gradually increase.

Make time to reinvent yourself.

DAY 20

Pity Party

The other side of pain is joy.

Life will continue to move on whether you want it to or not. You have the capability to move beyond *every* hurt, *every* pain.

It may appear like all is lost while you are in the moment of despair. Yet, if you think back to all the moments when you thought you were at your worst, you will realize you overcame those feelings. You triumphed over your pain and despair.

Each difficult moment in your life is just a speed bump to the next positive moment in your life. You cannot see or feel it while you are in the midst of your pain, but joy is right around the corner.

Allow yourself to feel the pain. It's okay. Don't try to be so strong that your emotions are buried. Feel every feeling …good or bad. Have a pity party. Keep it brief. Then begin to wipe the tears away and let the joy seep in.

Know that you will overcome this moment of sadness and look back on it as a lesson learned…a lesson of your true inner strength.

Have a PITY PARTY then move on!

DAY 21

Doors

Doors are meant to be opened and closed.

It is often said when one door closes, another door opens.

Take the time to close the doors to the past that caused pain and disappointment. Slam them shut and do not look back.

You will never forget the memories of what happened behind those closed doors, but you now have the opportunity to put the past in to perspective, learn from any mistakes, and move on.

The new doors can hold hope, joy, and the promise of something better.

Open the door to great possibilities!

DAY 22

Taking Me Time

Taking time for yourself can help you to refocus.

Sometimes life may appear to be overwhelming. We focus on helping everyone else and neglect the most important person – ME. It is okay to be there for everyone else but it is more important to take ME TIME.

Those closest to you will understand your need to be "alone" or "hibernate" for a while. It is not a long term vacation but a respite for YOU.

Take time to rejuvenate your mind, body, and spirit. Take time to focus on the inner peace that is often so elusive. Take time to find the peace within.

Why not start right now?

DAY 23

Your Today

It is often said that tomorrow is not promised...
so live for today.

Think about your TODAY.

It may be frustrating, difficult, and sad...yet it may also be satisfying, meaningful, and joyous.

Your today begins the moment you open your eyes.

You must choose how each day will flow. Obstacles may be in your path but you must choose whether to stop in your tracks or find another way around them.

People may frustrate you but you cannot change others...
only how you react to them.

Today take a deep breath, pause before speaking, enjoy each simple moment, and know it is your Today!

TODAY is yours... Choose how you live it!

DAY 24

Choices

Life is CHOICE driven. What choices are you making today?

Choose PEACE!

Choose LOVE!

Choose JOY!

Choose RESPECT!

Choose PATIENCE!

Choose and then choose again.

Each day, we have to reevaluate our lives and decide what is in our best interest. Some of our choices will take us to the depths of despair; while others will bring us to the heights of elation. Yet, choices are a part of life.

As you arise each day, choose to make this day better than the last.

The CHOICE is yours!

DAY 25

Emotional Bankruptcy

Sometimes we may fear letting go and hang on just because.

We must be honest with ourselves and allow our true emotions to reign. When we allow our emotions to spiral, we end up emotionally bankrupt. The empty vault of our heart aches for something more.

More honesty.

More trust.

More love.

When we try our very best to ensure the needs of others are met before our own, we lose ourselves. When we love so hard that it hurts, it truly hurts.

It is often difficult to see the shades of gray when the rose-colored glasses are on.

Take the glasses off. No more withdrawals. You can rebuild.

Begin by letting go and making *deposits* within!

DAY 26

Transition

Transition is a part of life.

Transition occurs when there is a change.

Change comes in many forms.

The most difficult transition is often the result of a loss. When it is the loss of someone you love, the transition pulls on your heart strings. The strings will stretch as you experience shock, denial, anger, guilt, bargaining, and depression. It may take a while for the tension in your heart strings to relieve the pressure to allow you to experience acceptance of the loss and eventually hope.

Allow yourself to experience all the emotions of the transition.

The heartstrings will recover in time.

DAY 27

The Power of Saying NO

NO is one of the most powerful words in your vocabulary.

NO is a complete sentence that needs no extra explanation.

When you learn to say NO to...

>...last minute requests

>...being taken advantage of

>...persistent people in your life

>...having that extra bite of your favorite food

>...will you? ...can you? ...I need you to...

...you begin to maximize your power.

Practice saying NO without guilt or a second thought.

It is very freeing!

DAY 28

Battered But NOT Broken

In life you may experience difficult situations.

You have the ability to overcome those difficult situations.

When you feel beat down and all strength appears to be gone, dig deep inside your soul and conjure up the strength from within.

It is there, lying dormant and waiting...

>...for you to access it

>...for you to realize you are a conqueror

>...for you to relinquish the pain and hurt

>...for you to rise up and realize

You CANNOT be BROKEN!

DAY 29

Un-Friending

Life is full of life cycles of beginnings and endings.

Friendships are like life cycles.

Some continue on through thick and thin; the bond strengthens over time.

However, others are held together because of insecurities, guilt, or fear of being alone.

Determine if your friendship is tied together with string or copper wire.

Is it unbreakable because it is a healthy relationship?

...or...

Is it breaking your heart because you know the life cycle is complete?

Take time away from friends to reevaluate your bond.

If the life cycle is complete, you must un-friend.

DAY 30

Stronger

The strength to overcome adversity is within us all.

Although your hard days may be behind you or just around the corner, your inner strength can topple grief, divorce, abuse, financial strain, broken friendships, broken promises, and so much more.

When enduring your pain and despair, it is often difficult to recognize your inner strength. Yet it is there, waiting for you to access it. Once accessed, you are able to breakthrough the pain and despair and grow.

With each day, LOVE stronger.
With each day, DREAM stronger.
With each day, LIVE stronger.
With each day,
BE
STRONGER!

Other Thoughts...

When life is raining down on you with pain, despair, and disappointment; open your umbrella of hope and possibility. Know there is a rainbow of joy on the other side.

Life is full of pleasant surprises. When you get one, sit back and enjoy the moment.

Don't confuse BITTER with DONE! Although others may consider your silence as BITTER, know in your heart you are DONE with, the situation, the drama, and the person. *(fill in the blank)*

The words that come out of your mouth will either be filled with hope or harm. Once they come out, they cannot be taken back.

You cannot wait for someone else to mend your broken heart. Pick up the pieces and put them back together with band-aids of self-love, hope, and forgiveness.

We all experience life. We all experience death. It is what happens in between that distinguishes us!

When love hurts, sometimes it is best to take a step back, reflect, and start over.

Be still! What you are searching for may actually be right in front of you.

If you take baby steps, you can climb out of the valley of despair!

Your choices in life will have an effect on those around you.

Each new day is filled with endless possibilities!

When all is said and done, YOU have a CHOICE...either LAY in the ashes of despair and pain or RISE above it. Not easy, but very doable!

All of the riches in the world cannot buy PEACE OF MIND. It must come from within.

Focus on what you HAVE and not what you DO NOT HAVE. It could all be gone in an instant.

Don't SETTLE because it is the EASY thing to do. Look deep within for the RIGHT thing to do.

May your day be filled with love. Start by loving yourself first!

Continue loving even through loss. Love NEVER fails.

Start checking off your bucket list while it is still a small pail. Tomorrow is NOT promised.

The weekend is yours to enjoy. Enjoy it to the fullest!

You are a conqueror of your circumstances. Vow not to repeat past mistakes.

Falling in love is easy. Staying in love is hard. If love is meant to be, you will find the balance.

Wake up with a smile and hold on to it all day!

When the rose-colored glasses come off, you may be blinded by a painful truth. As your vision clears, recognize the truth for what it is and take appropriate action to maintain your happiness.

Although it may be painful, sometimes you have to let it go. After the pain, there will be peace of mind.

For some, today may be the beginning of the new week. For others, today may be the beginning of a new life. Either way, make your today the beginning of new found peace and joy.

Refrain from spending another moment blaming life on your past. Be thankful for your past experiences. They made you stronger and wiser. Each day should now be filled with new hope and possibilities.

Stop being afraid of realizing your potential. Take a leap of faith and begin the journey to your potential today.

The storms of life are inevitable. The good news is the sun is always right around the corner waiting to shine! Today, dismiss the negatives in your life. Shine just because you can!

Start your day believing it will be great!
You have the power to make it a reality!

Do not hold on to people and things because it is easy or comfortable. Make a hard choice and let go and live! You will survive!

Renew your mind and let go of past hurts. You have the power to make each year an AWESOME year! Access your power!

Reflect on the year that was and know that each day was worth the trials and tribulations! You are wiser and stronger because of them!

Don't get caught up in the holiday gifting. Be sure to gift yourself something as well! You deserve it!

Claim each moment as your own personal victory! Good things are yours for the taking!

MAKE MY DAY! Don't wait for someone else to make your day! YOU have the power to make your day GOOD, BAD, or UGLY! Try it!

RISE and SHINE! As you wake up each day, know that you have the power to overcome anything! The possibilities are truly endless! Yes, you can RISE up and SHINE today!

Your challenges are only speed bumps on your path to greatness! Find a way around them or go over them slowly. There is always a lesson in the challenge.

JOY comes in the morning. Either choose to embrace it or allow it to slip through your fingers. What will you decide?

Wake up with the expectation of having a GOOD day and then choose to make it GREAT!

Great things are in store for you. BELIEVE in yourself and you will see the results!

You deserve to be PAMPERED. Pamper yourself! Don't wait for anyone else!

Enjoy the rain showers that may pour. If they are negative, learn how to open your own umbrella to shield yourself from the hurt. If they are positive, gather buckets to savor in the joy. Either way, welcome the rain showers and know a rainbow is always on the other side!

Life is Good. Be grateful for every *little* and *big* moment.

Enjoy EVERY single minute of today.
1,440 minutes to enjoy YOU!

Spend every weekend loving yourself. You deserve it!

LOVE on purpose and be KIND. Today nor tomorrow is promised.

RENEW your mind. Get rid of negative thoughts and negative people. It is so freeing!

Everyday is a great day to ENJOY life!

JOY comes in the morning!
Good morning JOY!

Today, be THANKFUL for the *little* things.

A POSITIVE attitude goes a long way! Try being positive today!

When the time springs forward, YOU have an extra hour to do great things.

Always allow your POSITIVE vibes to outweigh your NEGATIVE vibes!

Regardless of the distance or circumstances, if you have real, true love it will endure all things.

Today smile because you can.

Today laugh because you can.

Today be happy because you can.

Life is all about choices.

Manage your emotions. Don't allow others to manage them for you.

Why set STANDARDS if you are going to lower them for temporary gains? Know you are WORTHY of the STANDARDS you set in your life.

Know who you are. Love who you are. You don't have to change to please someone else.

The ability to FORGIVE will you give you PEACE of MIND!

Try it. FORGIVE! Let go. Enjoy the PEACE.

Give yourself two pats on the back today. You do not have to wait for others to validate you. Celebrate yourself!

Weed out all of the negative thoughts from your head and all the negative people from your life. It makes loving yourself so much easier.

When the mountain seems to high to climb, remember YOU have the POWER to turn the mountain into dust! Continue climbing until you reach your destination!

Sometimes we may fear hurting the feelings of others to the detriment of our own feelings.

A true friend will ground you through your insane moments and love you back to life when you think all hope is gone! Be thankful for real, true friendships!

Be YOURSELF. No one can do it better than YOU!

Make time to access your opportunities. Do not spend another day making excuses about the cant's in your life.

Walk on the sidewalk of love, hope, and joy today. Hop and skip over the cracks of hate, despair, and sadness *with a smile on your face.*

Stop trying to please everyone else.
TODAY, take time to please yourself.

Positive thinking plus positive actions equal a positive life.

ABOUT THE AUTHOR

Sonya L. Ford, Ed.D., is a Licensed Clinical Professional Counselor (LCPC) in private practice in Maryland. She received her BS from Old Dominion University, her MS from The Johns Hopkins University, and her EdD from The American School of Professional Psychology at Argosy University. A former radio personality; Dr. Sonya is currently a school counselor, adjunct professor, therapist, author, poet, and motivational speaker. She is the proud mother of two awesome children.

www.DrSonyaSays.com

CPSIA information can be obtained at www.ICGtesting.com
Printed in the USA
LVOW01s1634270913

354474LV00012B/370/P